The Coolest Pets

Fish

Anne O'Daly

KidHaven
PUBLISHING

Published in 2024 by
KidHaven Publishing, an Imprint of Greenhaven Publishing, LLC
2544 Clinton St., Buffalo, NY 14224

Copyright © 2019 Brown Bear Books Ltd

Portions of this work were originally authored by Dawn Titmus and published as *Fish*.
All new material this edition authored by Anne O'Daly.

Design Manager: Keith Davis
Picture Manager: Sophie Mortimer

Photo Credits:
Front Cover: Shutterstock: Mikhail Grigorev tl, Horath82 tr, Lotus Studio br, Alexander Potapov bl..
Interior: Dreamstime: Mikhailg 21b, 26–27; iStock: b_ial_y 20, EuToch 19t, FamVeld 11t, isoft 24, mtreasure 21t, rclassenlayouts 18, vlado1 14–15b, 15; Shutterstock: 12photography 10t, anmbph 9b, banosan 25t, Jovan Barajevac 12, bluehand 23b, Chaikom 4, cynoclub 4–5, 6, ET1972 7b, FamVeld 12-13, Sergii Figurny 5t, Elena Frolova 29l, Alexander Geiger 8-9t, Iliuta Goean 22, Lapis2380 13, CO Leong 14–15t, Kazakov Maksim 27t, Grigorev Mikhail 16, MyStocks 1, Krzysztof Odziomek 29b, Oleg_P 19b, Peyker 7t, Mirko Rosenau 10bl, 10br, 11b, 27b, Kocsis Sandor 23t, 25b, set 17t, showcake 9cr, Pavaphon Supanantananont 17b, Vlad61 29t, Suttipon Yakham 10c; Thinkstock: mauriziobiso 8–9b.
Key: t=top, b=bottom, c=centre, l=left, r=right

Cataloging-in-Publication Data

Names: O'Daly, Anne
Title: Fish / Anne O'Daly.
Description: Buffalo, New York : Kidhaven Publishing, 2024. |
Series: The coolest pets| Includes index and glossary
Identifiers: ISBN 9781534545298 (pbk) | ISBN 9781534545304 (library bound) | ISBN 9781534545311 (ebook)
Subjects: LCSH: Fish-- Juvenile literature |Fish as Pets--Juvenile literature |Pets--Juvenile literature
Classification: LCC SF457.25 O33 2024 | DDC 639.34--dc23

Manufactured in the United States of America

CPSIA compliance information: Batch #CSKH24: For further information contact Greenhaven Publishing LLC at 1-844-317-7404.

Please visit our website, www.greenhavenpublishing.com.
For a free color catalog of all our high-quality books, call toll free 1-844-317-7404 or fax 1-844-317-7405.

Find us on

Contents

Choosing a Fish

Fish are popular pets. They come in an amazing range of sizes and incredible colors. They are relaxing to watch and easy to care for.

Time and Space

Do you have time and space to keep and look after fish? The tank needs to be kept clean and the water changed regularly. The tank needs to be in the right place. You'll need a spot away from direct heat sources, such as a sunny window or radiator. It should be away from drafty areas. Place it on a firm, flat surface raised off the floor.

Tropical or Coldwater?

Tropical fish and coldwater fish have different care needs. Tropical fish, such as tetras, come from hot regions of the world. The water in their tank needs to be warm for the fish to survive. Goldfish are coldwater fish. They can live in water that is the same temperature as the rooms in most homes.

Checklist

✳ Do you want to keep coldwater or tropical fish?

✳ Have you researched how to look after the fish you want to keep?

✳ Do you have the space for a fish tank?

✳ Do you have time to clean the tank and change the water regularly?

✳ Can your family afford to buy the equipment?

A Community Aquarium

Some fish like to be with their own type of fish. Others can live with different species. When different fish are kept in one tank it is called a community aquarium. Guppies, southern platies, and mollies can all live happily with other types of fish.

Next Steps

Fish are great pets and are fascinating to watch, but it is important to choose the right ones for you. This book will help you to pick and care for your pet. Learn about six fish that are among the easiest to care for. Try your hand at making a Jello aquarium. You will also find some fascinating facts about your new fishy friends!

Getting Started

The most important piece of equipment is the tank. Think about what kind of fish you want to keep. That will determine the size of the tank, and whether the water needs to be heated.

The Tank

Once you have decided on the type of fish you want to keep, buy the biggest tank you can afford. Don't buy fish that will outgrow the tank. Start with a 20-gallon (75-liter) tank. Line the bottom of the tank with gravel. You will need a gravel cleaner (siphon set) for cleaning the tank.

Checklist

✳ The biggest tank you can afford.
✳ Heater and thermostat for tropical fish.
✳ A filter the right size for the tank.
✳ Tank ornaments and water plants.
✳ Tank gravel.
✳ Gravel cleaner (siphon set).
✳ Air pump (optional).

Tank

Plants and Decoration

Plants and ornaments in the tank look attractive and also provide shelter, hiding places, and shade for your fish. Some fish nibble on water plants, so you will have to replace the plants from time to time. Be sure to use aquatic ornaments that are safe for fish.

Filter and Air Pump

Filters help keep the water clean. They remove bits of uneaten food and fish poop. They stop harmful chemicals from building up. Set up a filter that is the right size for your tank. Change the filter material regularly. You can also install an air pump to get more oxygen into the water.

Temperature

Tropical fish need the water to be at higher temperatures than coldwater fish. Most tropical fish are happiest in water that is between 75 and 82°F (24 and 28°C). Use a heater with a thermostat to keep the water at the correct temperature for your fish.

Filter

Air pump

water heater

The Tank

It is important to prepare the tank properly before you bring any pet fish home. Clean the tank regularly to keep your fish healthy and happy in their new home.

Testing Kits

You can buy testing kits for the water at the pet store. Test the water for harmful chemicals before you add any fish. Some fish stores will test a sample of tank water for you. Test the water regularly when your tank contains fish. If the chemical levels are too high, you need to change the water.

Preparing the Tank

Water from the faucet contains chemicals that are harmful to fish. The tank filter also needs to grow some "good" bacteria. You can buy products at the pet store that remove chemicals from tap water and help good bacteria grow. Rinse the gravel with water and add it to the tank. Fill the tank with water and add the ornaments and plants. Turn on all the equipment. Run it for at least three days before you introduce fish to the tank. Make sure the water temperature is right for your type of fish.

Cleaning Up

Check all equipment every day. If there is uneaten food and waste in the tank, take it out with a net. Scrub off any algae growing on the side of the tank. Clean or change the filter regularly. Use water from the aquarium to wash the filter. Tap water contains bacteria that is harmful to fish. Never use any detergents to clean the tank as they can harm the fish.

Adding Air

Air pumps create bubbles. This moves the water around and gets more oxygen into the water, which is good for your fish. It's also fun to watch your fish swim through bubbles!

Siphon

Fresh Water

The tank water needs to be changed about once a week. Remove 15 to 20 percent of the water using a siphon. Top up the tank with water that has been treated to remove harmful chemicals.

Feeding

You will need to feed your pet fish regularly. Ask at the pet store which diet is best for your fish and how much to feed them. The right amount is important for your fish to stay healthy.

A Well-Balanced Diet

Give your fish other types of food as well as flakes for a balanced diet. Goldfish will eat chopped-up spinach or lettuce. Some types of tropical fish like crumbled egg yolk. Meat-eating fish, such as swordtails, need small live food, such as brine shrimp. You can also buy it frozen in fish stores.

Fish Food

Flakes

Pellets

Freeze-dried food

Fish food includes flakes and pellets for plant and meat eaters, and freeze-dried food. Some fish such as catfish feed from the bottom of the tank. They need food that will sink. Fish that feed at the surface, such as hatchetfish, need food that will float, such as flakes or floating pellets.

Just Right

Most fish need to be fed once or twice every day. Feed only as much as the fish eat in a few minutes. Giving your fish too much food is bad for them. Food that is uneaten will go stale, making the water unhealthy. Your filter system will have to work harder to keep the harmful bacteria from growing.

Check the Date

Check the sell-by date on fish food before you buy. Food that is out of date can lack vitamins. Keep the food in an airtight container, away from heat and light. Make sure no water gets into the container. Even a small amount of moisture can cause harmful bacteria to grow in the food.

Keeping Healthy

Good water quality will help keep your pet fish healthy. So will feeding the right food in the correct amount. But sometimes, fish get sick. Check your fish every day for signs of sickness.

Healthy Fish

Healthy fish eat their food and are active and alert. They have clear, bright eyes. The gills open and close regularly, and their fins do not have any splits or tears. Watch for signs of sickness in your fish. Take it to the vet if you think it is ill.

A New Home

Once the tank is all set up and working properly, you can slowly introduce the fish. Leave the fish in the bag you brought it home in. Float the bag in the tank so the fish gets used to the temperature. You can put a little of the tank water in the bag after about 20 minutes. After about 30 minutes, let the fish swim into the tank. Throw away the water that was in the bag.

Signs of Sickness

✳ Gasping at the surface.

✳ Swimming at an angle.

✳ Injuries or lumps on the scales.

✳ Pale patches on the scales.

✳ White spots.

✳ White tufts like cotton balls.

Plenty of Space

Be careful not to put too many fish into your tank. Overcrowding will stress the fish and can make them sick. Your filter will also have to work a lot harder to keep the water clean. A general rule is 1 inch (2.5 cm) of fish length per gallon (3.8 liters) of water. Plants and ornaments take up space, too. Put fewer fish in the tank than you think it can hold.

Carefully introduce fish to the tank.

A Happy Home

Check that the temperature of the water is right for your pet. Use a test kit to check for harmful chemicals and change the water regularly. Only leave tank lights on for 8 to 10 hours a day, not all the time. Fish need downtime!

Wild Fish

Fish live in fresh water, seawater, and brackish water, which is slightly salty. They are found all around the world. Most of the fish kept as pets in aquariums live in fresh water in the wild.

South America

Many types of aquarium fish come from South America. These include the tetras and red-bellied piranhas (right). Rivers and streams in South America range from clear, uncolored waters to the black water of the Rio Negro in the Amazon basin. Around 3,000 different types of fish live in the Amazon basin.

African Rift Lakes

The African Rift Lakes are in eastern Africa. They are among the largest and deepest lakes in the world. More than 1,500 different types of fish live in the lakes. Some, such as the Malawi golden cichlid, are found nowhere else in the world.

Friends and Enemies

Some fish, such as the dwarf gourami, live happily with other types of fish, as they would in the wild. Other fish are not suitable for a community aquarium. Oscars and angelfish (right) eat other smaller fish in the wild. Bettas (Siamese fighting fish) are territorial in the wild. Male bettas are very aggressive toward each other and should not be kept in the same tank. But bettas can be kept with peaceful fish, such as tetras.

Schooling Fish

In the wild, some fish, such as danios, swim together in groups, called schools. Individual fish in a large group have less chance of being eaten by a predator than if they are swimming alone. Schooling fish need to have tank mates of their own kind. If they are alone, they will become nervous and stressed. Schooling fish usually live happily with other types of fish in a community aquarium.

White Cloud Mountain Minnow

The White Cloud Mountain minnow is a sociable fish. This makes it ideal for a community aquarium. It is a good pet for beginners.

Where in the World?

The White Cloud Mountain minnow lives in streams in mountainous regions in southern China. It is rare in the wild today. A closely related fish was found in northeastern Vietnam in 2001.

The White Cloud Mountain minnow can live in a coldwater or tropical aquarium.

Pet Care

White Cloud Mountain minnows are schooling fish. Keep them in groups of at least five fish.

✳ They can live in water temperatures as low as 64°F (18°C) and up to about 72°F (22°C).

✳ They eat flakes with lots of vegetables and freeze-dried foods such as brine shrimp and blood worms.

Profile

The White Cloud Mountain minnow grows to about 1.75 inches (4.5 cm) long. An iridescent line runs along the body. Males have red-colored fins. There are gold and long-finned types. All types of minnows can live for up to four or five years.

Goldfish

Goldfish come in many sizes and colors. They have been kept by people for hundreds of years. Goldfish are one of the most popular pet fish.

Where in the World?

Goldfish come from China. They were first kept as pets about 1,000 years ago. They were taken to Japan in the 1500s and were introduced to Europe in the 1700s.

There are about 150 different types of goldfish.

Pet Care

Goldfish do not need a water heater unless the room is very cold. The water temperature can be between 65 and 77°F (18 and 25°C).

✽ Goldfish can live in a tank by themselves or with others. Comet and fancy goldfish are not good tank mates. The comets swim faster and get to the food first.

✽ Goldfish will eat most food types. Feed them good-quality flake or pellet made especially for goldfish.

Profile

The goldfish is a member of the carp family. Depending on the type, goldfish grow to about 12 inches (30 cm) long, but some are smaller. Fancy goldfish need greater care than common goldfish. Goldfish live for about six to eight years, but some may live much longer.

Neon Tetra

The tropical neon tetra has beautiful bright colors. It is one of the most popular pet fish. It is a peaceful fish and one of the easiest to care for.

Where in the World?

The neon tetra originally came from rivers and streams in rain forests in Colombia, Peru, and Brazil. It is often found in blackwater streams, where its bright colors make it stand out.

Neon tetras are known for their shimmering colors.

Pet Care

Neon tetras are schooling fish, so keep them in groups of at least five fish.

✳ Keep the water temperature in the tank at about 68 to 79°F (20 to 26°C).

✳ Neon tetras feed on regular flake food and pellets, as well as on frozen and live food.

Profile

The neon tetra has a silver-white body. It has a blue stripe that runs along its body from its nose to just past its back fin. It also has a red stripe that starts in the middle of the body and ends at the tail fin. Tetras grow to about 1.2 inches (3 cm) in length. Females are slightly larger than males. Neon tetras live for 10 or more years.

Molly Fish

Mollies are easy to care for and get along with others. They make great community aquarium fish. Female mollies give birth to live young rather than laying eggs.

where in the World?

In the wild, mollies live in freshwater streams and in brackish and coastal waters from Texas to Mexico. Some are found in waters in Colombia and Venezuela.

The molly is a good fish for a beginner.

Pet Care

Mollies like company. Keep at least one male and two females together, or a group of females if you don't want them to breed.

✳ The water in the tank can be fresh or brackish—with a little salt added. Keep the temperature around 77 to 82°F (25 to 28°C).

✳ Mollies will feed on algae, flakes, and frozen and dried food.

Profile

Mollies are available in many different colors, shapes, and patterns. The black molly is one of the most popular. Other types are the gold dust molly, which is yellow and orange, and the black-and-white dalmatian molly. Females grow to about 4.5 inches (12 cm), and males grow to 3 inches (8 cm). They live for three to five years.

Guppy

Guppies come in a huge range of colors, fin types, and patterns. They are active swimmers, making them fun to watch. The females give birth to live young.

where in the world?

Guppies live in the waters of Venezuela, Brazil, and some Caribbean islands. They eat insects and have been introduced to other parts of the world to try to reduce mosquito populations.

Guppies are also known as rainbow fish and millions fish.

Pet Care

Guppies are active tropical fish and need plenty of space to swim. They also like plants to nibble on.

* The temperature of the water should be around 64 to 82°F (18 to 28°C).

* Feed guppies flake food. Pellets are too large for their mouths. They also feed on live or frozen food such as brine shrimp.

Profile

Male guppies are more colorful than females, often with long, flowing tail fins. Guppy colors include yellow, red, blue, and purple. There are also patterned types such as snakeskin and lace guppies. Females grow to about 2 inches (5 cm) and are double the size of the males. Guppies live for three to five years.

Zebra Danio

Zebra danios are active, playful fish. They are fast swimmers and need enough space to move around. These fish make great pets for new owners.

Where in the World?

In the wild, zebra danios are found in rivers and streams of the Ganges Delta region in eastern India and Bangladesh.

The zebra danio gets its name from the stripes on its body, which look like zebra stripes.

Pet Care

Zebra danios like to live in a school of at least five fish. Good tank mates include rainbowfish, platies, mollies, and swordtails.

✳ The temperature of the water should be around 64 to 75°F (18 to 24°C).

✳ Feed zebra danios flake food and freeze-dried food such as blood worms and brine shrimp.

Profile

Zebra danios have dark horizontal stripes running the length of the body. Females are larger than males and have silver bodies. Males have gold bodies. Other types include the leopard danio (left), which has more spotted patterning, and some types have long fins. Danios grow to about 2 inches (5 cm) in length and live for about three to five years.

Easy-to-Make
Jello Aquarium

Use some Jello and candy to
make this fishy aquarium. Shine a light through it to see it at its best.
Then you can eat it!

You Will Need:

* Large glass bowl or clear plastic container
* 3 oz (85 g) packet of blue Jello powder
* 1 cup (250 ml) hot water
* 1.25 cups (315 ml) cold water
* Jelly beans or round gummies
* Fish-shaped gummy candy
* Green licorice or twisted candy

1 Ask an adult to help you mix the Jello powder with 1 cup of hot water. Add the cold water. You are using more water than listed on the Jello packet to make the Jello a lighter blue.

2 Place some jelly beans or gummies in the bottom of your container to look like gravel. Pour in the Jello mixture.

3 Put the container in the refrigerator for two hours, or until the Jello is just beginning to set.

4 Use a butter knife or skewer to make small holes in the Jello. Gently put the fish-shaped gummy candies in some of the holes.

5 Put some green licorice or candy strands in the remaining holes to look like water plants.

6 Return the container to the refrigerator for another two hours, or until the Jello has set.

Fun Facts

There are tens of thousands of different species of fish in the world today. Scientists are discovering new ones all the time.

The smallest fish is a carp that comes from Sumatra, in Indonesia. It is only about 0.3 inch (7.9 mm) long—about the size of your pinky fingernail!

Scientists have found that goldfish can be trained to link certain sounds with feeding time. They can even remember these sounds up to five months later.

Fish breathe by taking oxygen from the water. They take water into their mouths, where it passes over special organs called gills. The gills absorb oxygen from the water, which then passes into the fishes' bloodstream.

Scientists who study fish are called ichthyologists (ICK-thee-olo-jists).

Fish have been swimming in the oceans for about 450 million years!

Female seahorses lay their eggs in a pouch on the male's body. The eggs stay in the pouch for about 45 days, until they are ready to hatch.

The largest fish in the world is the whale shark. It can grow up to 40 feet (12 m) long. That's about the length of a school bus!

Glossary

algae plant or plantlike life-forms that grow mostly in water.

aquarium container, such as a glass tank, for water animals to live in.

aquatic relating to or living in water.

bacteria tiny life-forms that live in soil, water, and living things.

blood worms small, bright red worms used as fish food.

brackish slightly salty.

brine shrimp small shrimp used as fish food.

climate average weather conditions in a place or region over a period of years.

gills feathery parts of the body in fish that take oxygen from water.

iridescent displaying a range of rainbowlike colors.

oxygen gas in the air and water that people and animals need to live.

peaceful (of fish) not aggressive; will not bother tank mates.

siphon tube that uses air pressure to move liquid from one container to another.

sociable liking to be with others.

species group of animals or plants that are similar and are able to produce young.

territorial describes an animal that defends an area.

thermostat device that automatically controls temperature.

tropical occurring in or relating to the tropics– warm areas of the world close to the equator.

vitamin substance usually found in food that animals and people need to live and grow.

Further Resources

Books

Brainard, Jason. *Is a Fish a Good Pet for Me?* New York, NY: PowerKids Press, 2020.

Nugent, Samantha, and Jared Siemens. *Fish*. New York, NY: AV2, 2022.

Rossiter, Brienna. *My Pet Fish*. Mendota Heights, MN: Little Blue Readers, 2023.

Websites

Amazing World of Fish
easyscienceforkids.com/all-about-fish/
Learn more fun facts about fish!

Fish
kids.nationalgeographic.com/animals/fish
Discover wild fish from around the world.

Pet Fish
www.dkfindout.com/us/animals-and-nature/pet-care/pet-fish/
Explore helpful tips for keeping a pet fish happy and well.

Publisher's note to parents and teachers: Our editors have reviewed the websites listed here to make sure they're suitable for students. However, websites may change frequently. Please note that students should always be supervised when they access the internet.

Index